Light of the World
Leader Guide

D1160814

Light of the World
A Beginner's Guide to Advent

Light of the World
978-1-5018-8435-1
978-1-5018-8436-8 eBook

Light of the World DVD
978-1-5018-8430-6

Light of the World Leader Guide
978-1-5018-8438-2
978-1-5018-8439-9 eBook

AMY-JILL LEVINE

LIGHT *of* *the* WORLD

A BEGINNER'S GUIDE to ADVENT

LEADER GUIDE

by Maria Mayo

Abingdon Press
Nashville

LIGHT OF THE WORLD
A BEGINNER'S GUIDE TO ADVENT
LEADER GUIDE

Copyright © 2019 Abingdon Press
All rights reserved.

978-1-5018-8438-2

Scripture quotations unless noted otherwise are taken from the Common English Bible, copyright 2011. Used by permission. All rights reserved.

19 20 21 22 23 24 25 26 27 28 —10 9 8 7 6 5 4 3 2 1
MANUFACTURED IN THE UNITED STATES OF AMERICA

CONTENTS

TO THE LEADER

You are beginning a journey. As the leader of this study, you have the opportunity and responsibility to walk with a group of learners into the story at the beginning of the Christian experience—the story of Jesus' birth. You are not alone! You are going into this journey accompanied by a renowned biblical scholar who will help you and the group come to a deeper understanding of the texts and the traditions surrounding them. You also have this Leader Guide, which will give you all the ideas you need for four powerful learning sessions.

This Leader Guide is designed to be used with Amy-Jill Levine's book *Light of the World: A Beginner's Guide to Advent*. Dr. Levine, known to her friends, including you, as AJ, is University Professor of New Testament and Jewish Studies and Mary Jane Werthan Professor of Jewish Studies at Vanderbilt Divinity School and College of Arts and Sciences in Nashville, Tennessee. Besides being an accomplished author and scholar, AJ is a sought-after speaker who has given hundreds of talks both in the United States and internationally. She brings her Jewish background and her historical expertise in first-century Judaism and Christian origins to her work with the New Testament, and she opens insights into the connections between the Scriptures of Israel (what the church calls the "Old Testament") as well as postbiblical Jewish literature and the Gospels. She is also committed to helping present the Gospels as good news for all people, with a particular interest in what the Gospels say about women.

In this book, AJ brings her knowledge, her storytelling skills, and her own love of the Gospels to the story of the birth of Jesus. Looking at four different chapters in Matthew and Luke and looking as well at some of the pious, noncanonical stories of the Nativity, she unearths deep connections between the Jewish traditions and the events of Jesus' birth. She also helps set the cultural stage by drawing out how the Gospels address the political tensions in the early first century. AJ points out the emphases of Matthew and Luke as they tell the story, and how the chords sounded in the first two chapters of each Gospel can be heard throughout the rest of the text. She regards the distinct versions Matthew and Luke provide not as contradictions, but as variations on a theme, for the story of Jesus' birth cannot and should not be reduced to a singular perspective.

This Leader Guide provides you with the resources you need to lead this group. It's likely that you have more than enough material. So, you can choose from the options in the "Learning Together" sections to fit the time you have for your group meetings.

There are four sessions in this study, and it makes use of the following components:

- Amy-Jill Levine's book *Light of the World: A Beginner's Guide to Advent*,
- the DVD that accompanies the study, and
- this Leader Guide.

Participants in the study should plan on bringing Bibles and the *Light of the World* book to each session. If possible, notify those interested in the study in advance of the first session. Make arrangements for them to get copies of the book so they can read the introduction and chapter 1 before the first group meeting.

Using This Guide with Your Group

What will you find in this guide? A session format is below. It is designed to give you options and flexibility in planning your sessions with your group. You will want to develop your sessions with your group in mind, because different groups will have different interests as well as different dynamics. Choose any or all of the activities. Adapt. Reorder. Rearrange. Innovate. Here is the raw material for your lesson planning.

The session plans in this Leader Guide are designed to be completed in about 60 to 90 minutes, but you can use fewer activities to reduce the time to as little as 45 minutes. Depending on which activities you select, there may be special preparation needed. The session plan alerts the leader when advance preparation is required.

Session Format

Planning the Session

> Session Goals
> Scriptural Foundation
> Special Preparation

Getting Started

> Opening Activity
> Opening Prayer

Learning Together

> Video Study and Discussion
> Book and Bible Study and Discussion

Wrapping Up

> Closing Activity
> Closing Prayer

Optional Elements

Journaling

Journaling is a wonderful way to encourage more individual reflection and more extensive interaction outside the group sessions. You can promote the use of a journal by using one of your own as part of your preparation and class time. Group members can use any sort of book they would like for journaling, from a composition book to a bound, blank journal to sheets of loose-leaf paper. Some groups even use dedicated internet sites where they can post ideas and share thoughts. That approach gives you a permanent record of what you have learned and where you still have questions. Offer encouragement to those who decide to use the journal for reflecting on the reading, writing questions for future learning, and considering commitments they might make for their own spiritual growth. Some of the exercises suggested in the session plans can be done in the journal during class.

Connect with Your Church's Advent Traditions

Light of the World was created with the four weeks of Advent in mind. Invite your group members to take full part in the Advent and Christmas activities in your community of faith. Coordinate with your church leaders to develop a list of opportunities during the Advent season and consider going as a group to Advent services or Christmas activities.

Various communities will have a "walk through Bethlehem" experience—go to such a program after spending four weeks with this study, and you'll have a deeper appreciation for what you see.

You may also decide to watch a movie about the Nativity together or to look at paintings of the infant Jesus, the flight to Egypt, the Magi, and so forth—what do the artists and filmmakers add to the biblical stories?

Helpful Hints

Preparing for the Session

1. Pray. You are on an important journey. Pray for God's guidance as you discern and lead. Pray, as well, for the members of your group.
2. Before each session, familiarize yourself with the content. Read the book chapter again, and reread the Gospel passages on which the chapter is based. Take your time with the Gospel

reading; savor every word. If you can, read more than one translation. (AJ will guide you through translation issues.)

3. Depending on the length of time you have available for group meetings, you may or may not have time to do all the activities. Select the activities in advance that will work for your group time and interests.

4. Choose the session elements you will use during the group session, including the specific discussion questions you plan to cover. Be prepared, however, to adjust the session as group members interact and as questions arise.

5. Have your own sense of how you might respond to the questions, and if you wrestle with any of them, tell your group. Not all biblical passages lead to the same interpretation. We always bring to the text our own questions, and we always interpret based in part on our own experiences.

6. Prepare the room where the group will meet so that the space will enhance the learning process. Ideally, group members should be seated around a table or in a circle or semicircle so that all can see one another. Movable chairs are best because the group will sometimes be forming pairs or small groups for discussion.

7. Bring a supply of Bibles for those who forget to bring their own.

8. For most sessions you will also need a whiteboard and markers, or an easel with large sheets of paper and markers. You will also see suggestions for preparing large sheets of paper before the sessions.

Shaping the Learning Environment

- Begin and end on time.
- Create a climate of openness, encouraging group members to participate as they feel comfortable.
- Not all members of the group may know each other. Even if people do know each other, have them introduce themselves. They might share a joy or concern, they might talk about what

specifically interests them about the Nativity story (the story of the birth of Jesus), or they might share a Christmas memory or a question they've always had about the Gospel accounts.

- Nametags can be helpful, even in groups where everyone is supposed to know one another.

- Remember that some people will jump right in with answers and comments, while others need time to process what is being discussed.

- If you notice that some group members seem never to be able to enter the conversation, ask them if they have thoughts to share. Give everyone a chance to talk, but keep the conversation moving. Moderate to prevent a few individuals from doing all the talking.

- Communicate the importance of group discussions and group exercises.

- If no one answers at first during discussions, do not be afraid of silence. Count silently to ten, and then say something such as, "Would anyone like to go first?" If no one responds, venture an answer yourself and ask for comments.

- Model openness as you share with the group. Group members will follow your example. If you limit your sharing to a surface level, others will follow suit.

- You might share some questions you have of your own, which will help avoid the impression that you know everything (even if you do!).

- Encourage multiple answers or responses before moving on. Don't ask, "What does this story mean?"; ask, "What does this story mean *to you*?" You can assure them that there may be more than one good answer to a question, just as there is more than one way to tell the story of Jesus' birth.

- To help continue a discussion and give it greater depth, ask, "Why?" or "Why do you believe that?" or "Can you say more about that?"

- Affirm others' responses with comments such as "Great" or "Thanks" or "Good insight," especially if it's the first time someone has spoken during the group session.
- Monitor your own contributions. If you are doing most of the talking, back off so that you do not train the group to listen rather than speak up.
- Remember that you do not have all the answers. Your job is to keep the discussion going and encourage participation.

Managing the Session

- Honor the time schedule. If a session is running longer than expected, get consensus from the group before continuing beyond the agreed-upon ending time.
- Involve group members in various aspects of the group session, such as saying prayers or reading the Scripture.
- Note that the session guides sometimes call for breaking into smaller groups or pairs. This gives everyone a chance to speak and participate fully. Mix up the groups; don't let the same people pair up for every activity.
- As always in discussions that may involve personal sharing, confidentiality is essential. Group members should never pass along stories that have been shared in the group. Remind the group members at each session: confidentiality is crucial to the success of this study.

Chapter 1

THE MEANING OF MEMORY

Planning the Session

Session Goals

As a result of conversations and activities connected with this session, group members should begin to

- explore how these stories allow us to see the world in a new way,
- understand the Old Testament contexts for the story of Zechariah and Elizabeth,
- see how the story of the birth of John the Baptist prepares the way for Jesus, and
- appreciate the colorful humor in Zechariah's story (many people have been taught that there is nothing humorous in the Bible; this section can remind them that these are stories told not only to bring joy but also to evoke laughter).

Scriptural Foundation

During the rule of King Herod of Judea there was a priest named Zechariah who belonged to the priestly division of Abijah. His wife Elizabeth was a descendant of Aaron. They

were both righteous before God, blameless in their observance
of all the Lord's commandments and regulations. They had no
children because Elizabeth was unable to become pregnant
and they both were very old. One day Zechariah was serving
as a priest before God because his priestly division was on
duty. Following the customs of priestly service, he was chosen
by lottery to go into the Lord's sanctuary and burn incense.
All the people who gathered to worship were praying outside
during this hour of incense offering. An angel from the Lord
appeared to him, standing to the right of the altar of incense.
When Zechariah saw the angel, he was startled and overcome
with fear.

The angel said, "Don't be afraid, Zechariah. Your prayers have
been heard. Your wife Elizabeth will give birth to your son
and you must name him John. He will be a joy and delight to
you, and many people will rejoice at his birth, for he will be
great in the Lord's eyes. He must not drink wine and liquor.
He will be filled with the Holy Spirit even before his birth.
He will bring many Israelites back to the Lord their God. He
will go forth before the Lord, equipped with the spirit and
power of Elijah. He will turn the hearts of fathers back to their
children, and he will turn the disobedient to righteous patterns
of thinking. He will make ready a people prepared for
the Lord."

Zechariah said to the angel, "How can I be sure of this? My
wife and I are very old."

The angel replied, "I am Gabriel. I stand in God's presence.
I was sent to speak to you and to bring this good news to you.
Know this: What I have spoken will come true at the proper
time. But because you didn't believe, you will remain silent,
unable to speak until the day when these things happen."

Meanwhile, the people were waiting for Zechariah, and they
wondered why he was in the sanctuary for such a long time.
When he came out, he was unable to speak to them. They

*realized he had seen a vision in the temple, for he gestured
to them and couldn't speak. When he completed the days
of his priestly service, he returned home. Afterward, his
wife Elizabeth became pregnant. She kept to herself for five
months, saying, "This is the Lord's doing. He has shown his
favor to me by removing my disgrace among other people." . . .*

*When the time came for Elizabeth to have her child, she gave
birth to a boy. Her neighbors and relatives celebrated with her
because they had heard that the Lord had shown her great
mercy. On the eighth day, it came time to circumcise the child.
They wanted to name him Zechariah because that was his
father's name. But his mother replied, "No, his name will
be John."*

*They said to her, "None of your relatives have that name."
Then they began gesturing to his father to see what he wanted
to call him.*

*After asking for a tablet, he surprised everyone by writing, "His
name is John." At that moment, Zechariah was able to speak
again, and he began praising God.*

Luke 1:5-25, 57-64

Special Preparation

- If you are not in a room with a large table, prepare the room
  with seating arranged in a circle or semicircle so that everyone
  will be able to see one another.
- Have nametags available as well as pens and markers for the
  tags.
- Have available paper, pens, pencils, and other drawing
  materials.
- Also have available large sheets of paper or a whiteboard with
  markers for writing.
- Provide Bibles for those who may not have brought one.
  Encourage participants to bring a Bible for future sessions.

Although *Light of the World* uses the Common English Bible (CEB), let participants know that they can bring whatever version they have (NRSV, NIV, KJV, and so on); sometimes it is helpful to share different translations. You can remind them that the New Testament is written in Greek, so that all translations are approximations, and that the same term can be translated in different ways.

Getting Started

Opening Activity

Recalling the Events of Jesus' Birth

As participants arrive, greet them and invite them into a circle of chairs or to the table. Especially if you are working with a newly formed group, have all the participants write their names on a nametag and put it on. Begin the session with brief introductions.

Tell the group that this study will explore the stories around the birth of Jesus and the beginning of his earthly life. In these four sessions, we will look closely at Matthew's and Luke's (different!) accounts of Jesus birth and explore what we know and don't know about the Nativity traditions.

Ask the group members to share, without looking in the study book or a Bible, the events around Jesus' birth as they can remember them. You can start them off with an example, such as "the angel Gabriel," "census," or "manger." As participants share, write their responses on a large piece of paper titled "Events of Jesus' Birth" posted in a visible spot in the room. After the exercise, save this paper for use in a future session.

If you have time, ask them for a second list of Christmas associations, as in, "When I think of Christmas, I think about . . ." You might start with "holly and ivy," "Christmas trees," or "Yule log." Make a list. You can keep this list as well, to see how many of the items appear in the Gospels.

Opening Prayer

Pray together, using the following prayer or one of your own choosing:

God of our past, present, and future, bless our time together over the next few weeks. Guide us as we learn and draw inspiration from those who came before us. Help us live into the memory of all the ways that you enter into the world, and help us see the world in a new way in light of the stories of Jesus' birth. May we benefit from the wisdom of your people and your word. Amen.

Learning Together

Video Study and Discussion

Introduce the group to Amy-Jill Levine, author and host of the study, and professor of New Testament and Jewish Studies at Vanderbilt University. AJ has done more than five hundred programs for churches, clergy groups, and seminaries, and is the author of numerous books, including *The Misunderstood Jew: The Church and the Scandal of the Jewish Jesus* and *Entering the Passion of Jesus: A Beginner's Guide to Holy Week*. Make a point of telling the group how excited you are to be engaging AJ's work in this Advent study.

Play the first track on the *Light of the World* DVD: "Session 1: The Meaning of Memory" (running time is 9:54 minutes).

After the video session plays, invite discussion and questions from the group. To spark conversation, ask group members to consider this excerpt from the video session and the questions that follow:

> *The Lukan Christmas story is filled with remarkable news—unexpected, but urgently wanted, hoped-for news. Zechariah is told that his elderly, infertile wife will bear a child. Mary is told that she will have a child even though she has not yet had sexual relations. We are told that this newborn baby will be a Lord. Mary's Magnificat, her hymn, sings about status reversal past, present, and future. Magi see a star, the good news of the birth of a new king. . . . We have to be open to staggering news and rather than just*

say, oh, that can't possibly happen, rather than have doubt. One of the beauties of the Gospels is they help us envision the world otherwise; see the world differently.

- How is the Christmas story one of "staggering good news"?
- What does it say to us about being open to surprises and a "world otherwise"?
- What other parts of the video stood out to you?
- What did you learn about the early parts of Luke's story that you didn't already know?

Book and Bible Study and Discussion

Imagining Zechariah and Gabriel

Invite two members of the group to take on the roles of Gabriel and Zechariah. Using Luke 1:10-20 as a script, act out the encounter between the priest and the angel. AJ imagines that Gabriel is "huffy," saying, "Who are you to doubt me?"

"In antiquity," AJ writes, "the Gospel was not read by most people, in part because copying books was expensive, and in part because most people were illiterate. Instead, the Gospel was performed. We can picture the speaker, demonstrating angelic exasperation, wondering how he will deal with this obtuse priest."

Following the performance, consider the questions below:

- What is an annunciation? What are the essential characteristics?
- What are the central points of the annunciation to Zechariah?
- What are the various reasons this story takes place in the Temple? Do you imagine hearing the divine word differently when you are in church rather than when you are at home, or at a mall, or in a forest? How does setting enhance or detract from receiving God's word?

- We often ask God to speak to us. What do we think we would do if we had an angelic encounter? Can we even imagine it?
- John is to prepare this people for an intimate encounter with God. What would such preparation look like today, in the home or in the church? If you knew such an encounter was about to happen, what would you do, or do differently?

Jewish Stories

Invite the group to consider the following passage from the introduction to *Light of the World*:

> I regard these Gospel stories as Jewish stories and so part of my own history. Matthew and Luke quote Jewish sources, draw on Jewish images, are set in the Jewish homeland, and describe a Jewish messiah. If we miss that context, we'll also miss much of the message.

Ask the following questions:

- What do you know about Jewish history? Do you think of the "Old Testament" as a collection of books also shared with the Jewish community? Have you ever been to a synagogue?
- What are the Old Testament stories you remember best, and do you think they shed any new light on the Christmas stories?
- AJ tells us that the name Zechariah comes from the Hebrew word for "Remember." What events in your history, or church history, or world history, do you want the next generation to remember, and why?

The New Elijah

Ask a member of the group to read each of these two prophecies, one from Malachi about the return of Elijah (Malachi 4:5-6) and one from Gabriel instructing Zechariah about the mission of John the Baptist (Luke 1:16-17). Then consider the questions that follow.

The Prophet Malachi:

> *Look, I am sending Elijah the prophet to you,*
> *before the great and terrifying day of the* LORD
> *arrives.*
> *Turn the hearts of the parents to the children*
> *and the hearts of the children to their parents.*
> *Otherwise, I will come and strike the land with*
> *a curse.*
>
> *Malachi 4:5-6*

Gabriel to Zechariah:

> *"He will bring many Israelites back to the Lord their God.*
> *He will go forth before the Lord, equipped with the spirit and*
> *power of Elijah. He will turn the hearts of fathers back to their*
> *children, and he will turn the disobedient to righteous patterns*
> *of thinking. He will make ready a people prepared for the Lord."*
>
> *Luke 1:16-17*

- How are the words from Gabriel to Zechariah a rereading of the prophecy of Malachi?
- What does Luke add to the prophecy? What does Luke omit?
- How is John the Baptist "equipped with the spirit and power of Elijah"?
- In the Gospel of John (1:21), John the Baptist says that he is not Elijah. How is John both like, and unlike, Elijah? Do you remember any of the Elijah stories? How might knowing them help us better understand John?
- If you had to list "righteous patterns of thinking" (the Greek is "the wisdom of the righteous"), what would be on your list?
- How does the church help prepare its people to be ready for their Lord?

Benedictus

Read aloud Zechariah's song, known as the "Benedictus" (Latin for the first word of the song, "bless"). Zechariah is no longer silent!

> *"Bless the Lord God of Israel*
> > *because he has come to help and has delivered his*
> > *people.*
> *He has raised up a mighty savior for us in his servant*
> *David's house,*
> > *just as he said through the mouths of his holy*
> > *prophets long ago.*
> *He has brought salvation from our enemies*
> > *and from the power of all those who hate us.*
> *He has shown the mercy promised to our ancestors,*
> > *and remembered his holy covenant,*
> > > *the solemn pledge he made to our ancestor*
> > > *Abraham.*
> *He has granted that we would be rescued*
> > *from the power of our enemies*
> > *so that we could serve him without fear,*
> > > *in holiness and righteousness in God's eyes,*
> > > *for as long as we live.*
> *You, child, will be called a prophet of the Most High,*
> > *for you will go before the Lord to prepare his way.*
> *You will tell his people how to be saved*
> > *through the forgiveness of their sins.*
> *Because of our God's deep compassion,*
> > *the dawn from heaven will break upon us,*
> > *to give light to those who are sitting in darkness*
> > *and in the shadow of death,*
> > > *to guide us on the path of peace."*
> > > > *Luke 1:68-79*

• In the study book, AJ writes, "Luke tells us that Zechariah, filled with the Spirit (of course), 'prophesied' (1:67) and in doing so provides the assurance that, despite the newness of the Christmas story, a rock-solid base provides an anchor. God is invested in history, from the international level to the personal one." How does Zechariah's song demonstrate this investment? When you think of God, do you think of heaven or earth or both? Do you see God active not only in your own life, but also in history?

- For what actions is Zechariah praising God? What do you think he was expecting to see and to happen?
- What does Zechariah insist about God's covenant with Abraham and Israel?
- What does the "path of peace" look like? How do we know when we are walking on it?

Communicating in Silence

Divide the class into pairs. Instruct each pair to stay silent for two minutes. During that time, they should take turns using only hand gestures to explain an important Bible story or event. Each partner should try to decipher what is being described. When they are finished, have each pair exchange guesses and then use words to reveal the intended story.

At the end of the activity, reflect as a group on these questions:

- What was it like to try to explain something important without speaking?
- In acting out the event, did you laugh?
- Was it a relief finally to be able to talk about something so important?
- Do motions or images give a different impression than words? When you learn of a major event, do you think first of words or of images?
- Are there any events that are "unspeakable"?
- In what ways can silence be valuable? In our culture, what opportunities do we have to sit in silence, especially with other people?

Wrapping Up

Closing Activity

Essential Characters

As you reflect on the story of Elizabeth and Zechariah, think about the following questions as a group:

- How familiar were you with the stories of Zechariah and Elizabeth?
- When we tell the story of Jesus' birth, where do we usually begin? Where should we begin? Why do you think Luke chose to begin his Gospel with Zechariah and Elizabeth, and not with Mary and Joseph?
- What do we lose if we leave Zechariah and Elizabeth out of the story? What do they add, both literally and symbolically, to the good news?
- Zechariah and Elizabeth represent communal memory, the older people in the family, the aging of bodies, and the sense that waiting and waiting may never find a goal. What is lost when older people are not recognized for their gifts and not appreciated for their hopes?

Closing Prayer

If the group is using a common biblical translation, invite them to read aloud Psalm 40:5. Alternatively, ask a member of the group to read it aloud.

> *You, Lord my God!*
> *You've done so many things—*
> *your wonderful deeds and your plans for us—*
> *no one can compare with you!*
> *If I were to proclaim and talk about all of them,*
> *they would be too numerous to count!*
> *Psalm 40:5*

God of Advent and Christmas, thank you for coming into our world through the story of Elizabeth and Zechariah. Let us hope with their faithful hope for what may seem impossible. We are thankful for your many gifts and sing your praise! As we travel through this season, let us be mindful of your presence and your will. You who hear the prayers of all, lead us in peace. Amen.

Session 2

THE PROMISE OF POTENTIAL

Planning the Session

Session Goals

As a result of conversations and activities connected with this session, group members should begin to

- explore the connections between Mary and Hannah through their songs of praise and so enrich their understandings of both women,
- think about the pregnancy of Mary and the physicality of Jesus' birth in new ways,
- consider what it might mean for Mary and Elizabeth to be the mothers of children who will do extraordinary things and who will both be executed by political authorities, and
- reflect on time in a new way.

Scriptural Foundation

When Elizabeth was six months pregnant, God sent the angel Gabriel to Nazareth, a city in Galilee, to a virgin who was engaged to a man named Joseph, a descendant of David's house. The virgin's name was Mary. When the angel came

to her, he said, "Rejoice, favored one! The Lord is with you!"
She was confused by these words and wondered what kind of
greeting this might be. The angel said, "Don't be afraid, Mary.
God is honoring you. Look! You will conceive and give birth
to a son, and you will name him Jesus. He will be great and
he will be called the Son of the Most High. The Lord God
will give him the throne of David his father. He will rule over
Jacob's house forever, and there will be no end to his kingdom."

Then Mary said to the angel, "How will this happen since I
haven't had sexual relations with a man?"

The angel replied, "The Holy Spirit will come over you and
the power of the Most High will overshadow you. Therefore,
the one who is to be born will be holy. He will be called God's
Son. Look, even in her old age, your relative Elizabeth has
conceived a son. This woman who was labeled 'unable to
conceive' is now six months pregnant. Nothing is impossible
for God."

Then Mary said, "I am the Lord's servant. Let it be with me
just as you have said." Then the angel left her.

Mary got up and hurried to a city in the Judean highlands.
She entered Zechariah's home and greeted Elizabeth. When
Elizabeth heard Mary's greeting, the child leaped in her womb,
and Elizabeth was filled with the Holy Spirit. With a loud
voice she blurted out, "God has blessed you above all women,
and he has blessed the child you carry. Why do I have this
honor, that the mother of my Lord should come to me? As soon
as I heard your greeting, the baby in my womb jumped for
joy. Happy is she who believed that the Lord would fulfill the
promises he made to her."

Mary said,

> "With all my heart I glorify the Lord!
>   In the depths of who I am I rejoice in God my
>   savior.

> He has looked with favor on the low status of his
> servant.
>> Look! From now on, everyone will consider me
>> highly favored
>>> because the mighty one has done great things
>>> for me.
> Holy is his name.
>> He shows mercy to everyone,
>>> from one generation to the next,
>>> who honors him as God.
> He has shown strength with his arm.
>> He has scattered those with arrogant thoughts and
>> proud inclinations.
>> He has pulled the powerful down from their thrones
>>> and lifted up the lowly.
> He has filled the hungry with good things
>> and sent the rich away empty-handed.
> He has come to the aid of his servant Israel,
>> remembering his mercy,
>> just as he promised to our ancestors,
>>> to Abraham and to Abraham's descendants forever."

*Mary stayed with Elizabeth about three months, and then
returned to her home.*

Luke 1:26-56

Special Preparation

- Prepare the room with seating arranged in a circle, a semicircle, or around a table so that everyone will be able to see one another.
- Have nametags for all returning as well as new members.
- Have available paper, pens, pencils, and other drawing materials.
- Also have available large sheets of paper or a whiteboard with markers for writing.
- Provide Bibles for those who may not have brought one.

• If you have access to Bible dictionaries, have them available for participants to use.

Getting Started

Opening Activity

Envisioning Mary

You might have the group introduce themselves again. This will be helpful especially for new members. As they introduce themselves, they might speak to one of the images of Mary they have encountered, whether from Scripture, movies, Nativity scenes, icons, or stories.

Have the group name the characteristics of Mary as they have understood her. Was she peaceful? rebellious? with Joseph? alone? scared? calm? How old was she? What did she look like? Make a list on a large sheet of paper of all of the words the group associates with Mary. Set the paper aside to revisit at the end of the session.

Opening Prayer

Read the following prayer aloud or one of your own:

God of the Annunciation, bring us the good news of Christ's coming in our lives. Lead us through this study into greater understanding of your presence with us. Bless the work of our hands and grant us grace and kindness to gather with joy during this Advent season. Amen.

Learning Together

Video Study and Discussion

Play the second track on the *Light of the World* DVD: "Session 2: The Promise of Potential" (running time is 13:12 minutes).

After the video session plays, invite discussion and questions from the group. To spark conversation, ask group members to consider this excerpt from the video session about differences in translation of Isaiah 7:14 and the questions that follow:

Who got it right? The synagogue reading in the Hebrew got it right. The church reading in the Greek got it right as well. Because in religion, unlike elementary school mathematics, you can have two competing, in fact opposite, views and theologically, you can both be correct.

- What do you think of AJ's statement? Is it possible for people to translate a text differently and both be correct?
- When we interpret the Bible, do we all always find the same interpretation? Have you ever seen new things in a biblical text?
- Can opposite views both be correct?
- What other parts of the video stood out to you?
- What did you learn about Mary's experience that you didn't already know?

Book and Bible Study and Discussion

Mary and Miriam

In the study book, AJ discusses the symbolic value of Mary's name, and especially the connection between Mary and Miriam, the sister of Moses. Have a member of the group read out loud the story of Miriam and the baby Moses in Exodus 2:1-10. Consider as a group the questions that follow.

> *Now a man from Levi's household married a Levite woman. The woman became pregnant and gave birth to a son. She saw that the baby was healthy and beautiful, so she hid him for three months. When she couldn't hide him any longer, she took a reed basket and sealed it up with black tar. She put the child in the basket and set the basket among the reeds at the riverbank. The baby's older sister stood watch nearby to see what would happen to him.*

> *Pharaoh's daughter came down to bathe in the river, while her women servants walked along beside the river. She saw the basket among the reeds, and she sent one of her servants to bring it to her. When she opened it, she saw the child. The boy*

was crying, and she felt sorry for him. She said, "This must be one of the Hebrews' children."

Then the baby's sister said to Pharaoh's daughter, "Would you like me to go and find one of the Hebrew women to nurse the child for you?"

Pharaoh's daughter agreed, "Yes, do that." So the girl went and called the child's mother. Pharaoh's daughter said to her, "Take this child and nurse it for me, and I'll pay you for your work." So the woman took the child and nursed it. After the child had grown up, she brought him back to Pharaoh's daughter, who adopted him as her son. She named him Moses, "because," she said, "I pulled him out of the water."

Exodus 2:1-10

- AJ notes that names have meaning. Were you named after someone? Did you name your children after someone? What hopes did you, or your parents, have in this naming process?
- What light does the story of Miriam shed on Mary's experience?
- What does the Exodus story about collaboration of all these unnamed women—Moses' mother and sister, Pharaoh's daughter, the women attending Pharaoh's daughter—suggest about unnamed women who work together for human wholeness? Why do you think the Bible is so interested in telling stories about women?
- When Jesus is an adult, what role does his mother Mary play? What other stories about Mary do you remember? Are there parallels with Miriam?
- AJ writes, "Miriam is remembered primarily as poet and prophet and protector, and not as wife and mother. Mary, the mother of Jesus, is remembered primarily because of her son, but her motherhood is not her only characteristic. She, too, is poet and prophet and protector." In what ways are both Miriam and Mary "poet and prophet and protector"?

Mary Visits with Elizabeth

Read the following passage out loud and respond to the questions that follow.

> *Mary got up and hurried to a city in the Judean highlands. She entered Zechariah's home and greeted Elizabeth. When Elizabeth heard Mary's greeting, the child leaped in her womb, and Elizabeth was filled with the Holy Spirit. With a loud voice she blurted out, "God has blessed you above all women, and he has blessed the child you carry. Why do I have this honor, that the mother of my Lord should come to me? As soon as I heard your greeting, the baby in my womb jumped for joy. Happy is she who believed that the Lord would fulfill the promises he made to her."*
>
> Luke 1:39-45

- Elizabeth's words to Mary mark the first time in Luke's Gospel that anyone is called "blessed." Have you ever called anyone "blessed" or has anyone called you "blessed"? What might that label have meant?
- How did Elizabeth know that the Lord had made promises to Mary, and that Mary believed them?
- Both Mary and Elizabeth were first-time moms, together during a time of preparation. What do you think they talked about?
- Zechariah is mute in this scene, and Joseph is missing. What might they have been thinking?

Comparing the Good News

Luke describes an annunciation to Mary by the angel Gabriel (Luke 1:26-38), and Matthew describes Joseph's dream, in which an angel tells him that his fiancée, Mary, is having a baby (Matthew 1:18-23). What are the distinct messages that Mary and Joseph hear? If we only had one account, what would we be missing?

Mary:

> When Elizabeth was six months pregnant, God sent the angel
> Gabriel to Nazareth, a city in Galilee, to a virgin who was
> engaged to a man named Joseph, a descendant of David's
> house. The virgin's name was Mary. When the angel came
> to her, he said, "Rejoice, favored one! The Lord is with you!"
> She was confused by these words and wondered what kind of
> greeting this might be. The angel said, "Don't be afraid, Mary.
> God is honoring you. Look! You will conceive and give birth
> to a son, and you will name him Jesus. He will be great and
> he will be called the Son of the Most High. The Lord God
> will give him the throne of David his father. He will rule over
> Jacob's house forever, and there will be no end to his kingdom."
>
> Then Mary said to the angel, "How will this happen since I
> haven't had sexual relations with a man?"
>
> The angel replied, "The Holy Spirit will come over you and
> the power of the Most High will overshadow you. Therefore,
> the one who is to be born will be holy. He will be called God's
> Son. Look, even in her old age, your relative Elizabeth has
> conceived a son. This woman who was labeled 'unable to
> conceive' is now six months pregnant. Nothing is impossible
> for God."
>
> Then Mary said, "I am the Lord's servant. Let it be with me
> just as you have said." Then the angel left her.
>
> Luke 1:26-38

Joseph:

> This is how the birth of Jesus Christ took place. When Mary
> his mother was engaged to Joseph, before they were married,
> she became pregnant by the Holy Spirit. Joseph her husband
> was a righteous man. Because he didn't want to humiliate
> her, he decided to call off their engagement quietly. As he was
> thinking about this, an angel from the Lord appeared to him

*in a dream and said, "Joseph son of David, don't be afraid
to take Mary as your wife, because the child she carries was
conceived by the Holy Spirit. She will give birth to a son, and
you will call him Jesus, because he will save his people from
their sins." Now all of this took place so that what the Lord
had spoken through the prophet would be fulfilled:*

> *Look! A virgin will become pregnant and give birth to a
> son,*
> > *And they will call him, Emmanuel.*

(Emmanuel means "God with us.")

Matthew 1:18-23

- What does each version of the annunciations contribute to our understanding of Jesus' beginnings?
- What does each contribute to our picture of Mary and Joseph?
- Do you think Mary and Joseph talked about their angelic encounters? What did they say?

Maria Gravida

Maria gravida is Latin for "pregnant Mary." Images and icons with this label celebrate the visibly pregnant body of Mary. Before the session, search for images of "Maria Gravida" online and print out a few pictures for the group to consider. Pass the images around and ask the following questions:

- How does it feel to see Mary's pregnant body? Do we usually see Mary with a "baby bump"?
- How do we usually regard or treat women who are pregnant?
- What does it mean for the Divine to come into the world in such a visceral, physical way?
- How does looking at a pregnant Mary change or enhance how you see other pregnant women? your spouse? yourself?

Mary's Magnificat and Hannah's Song

AJ writes, "It is to Elizabeth that Mary sings the song traditionally called the Magnificat, the song that begins, 'With all my heart I glorify the Lord!' (Luke 1:46). Mary sings not only of divine glory; she sings also of ancient promises of social revolution. She sings the songs of Miriam and Deborah and Hannah, but in a new key for a new time."

Mary's Magnificat echoes Hannah's Song in both form and theme, celebrating the strength and steadfastness of God. Have a member of the group read Hannah's Song out loud, and then ask another group member to read Mary's Magnificat. Optional: Create a handout with two columns side by side, one for each song.

Hannah's Song

> *My heart rejoices in the LORD.*
>> *My strength rises up in the LORD!*
>> *My mouth mocks my enemies*
>>> *because I rejoice in your deliverance.*
> *No one is holy like the LORD—*
>> *no, no one except you!*
>> *There is no rock like our God!*
>
> *Don't go on and on, talking so proudly,*
>> *spouting arrogance from your mouth,*
>> *because the LORD is the God who knows,*
>>> *and he weighs every act.*
>
> *The bows of mighty warriors are shattered,*
>> *but those who were stumbling now dress themselves*
>> *in power!*
> *Those who were filled full now sell themselves for bread,*
>> *but the ones who were starving are now fat from food!*
>> *The woman who was barren has birthed seven*
>> *children,*
>>> *but the mother with many sons has lost them all!*

The L<small>ORD</small>!
>   *He brings death, gives life,*
>>   *takes down to the grave, and raises up!*

The L<small>ORD</small>!
He makes poor, gives wealth,
>   *brings low, but also lifts up high!*

God raises the poor from the dust,
>   *lifts up the needy from the garbage pile.*

God sits them with officials,
>   *gives them the seat of honor!*

The pillars of the earth belong to the L<small>ORD</small>;
>   *he set the world on top of them!*

God guards the feet of his faithful ones,
>   *but the wicked die in darkness*
>>   *because no one succeeds by strength alone.*

The L<small>ORD</small>!
His enemies are terrified!
>   *God thunders against them from heaven!*

The L<small>ORD</small>!
He judges the far corners of the earth!

May God give strength to his king
>   *and raise high the strength of his anointed one.*

1 Samuel 2:1-10

Mary's Magnificat

> *"With all my heart I glorify the Lord!*
>>   *In the depths of who I am I rejoice in God my*
>   *savior.*

> *He has looked with favor on the low status of his*
> *servant.*

>>   *Look! From now on, everyone will consider me*
>>   *highly favored*
>>>   *because the mighty one has done great things*
>>   *for me.*

37

> *Holy is his name.*
> > *He shows mercy to everyone,*
> > > *from one generation to the next,*
> > > *who honors him as God.*
> *He has shown strength with his arm.*
> > *He has scattered those with arrogant thoughts and*
> > *proud inclinations.*
> > *He has pulled the powerful down from their thrones*
> > > *and lifted up the lowly.*
> *He has filled the hungry with good things*
> > *and sent the rich away empty-handed.*
> *He has come to the aid of his servant Israel,*
> > *remembering his mercy,*
> > *just as he promised to our ancestors,*
> > > *to Abraham and to Abraham's descendants*
> > > *forever."*

Luke 1:46-55

- Notice the striking similarities between the two songs. Can you name the places where they agree?
- Are there messages about God that you think bear repeating?
- What does Mary's Magnificat tell us about how familiar she must have been with Scripture?
- How does Mary sing this song "in a new key for a new time"?
- Do you recall any songs that, today, sound similar themes, whether protest songs (for example: "If I Had a Hammer," "We Shall Overcome," "Blowin' in the Wind") or patriotic songs or church hymns?
- How do these songs resemble those of Miriam and Deborah and Judith?

Wrapping Up

Closing Activity

Take out the large sheet of paper from the opening activity. Look over the words contributed by the group, and ask participants to think about their images of Mary based on the information in chapter 2 of the study book. Would they change or add to any of the words included on the list? What "image" of Mary would they construct based on what they learned in the session?

Closing Prayer

Offer the following prayer or one of your own:

Come, Jesus. Make us aware of your light shining in everyone we meet. Give us the trust of Mary and Joseph to be open to your word and your will. May your strength and comfort be with all expectant mothers, in this season and always. Grant us insight into where you would have us go and what you would have us do. Amen.

Session 3

THE JOURNEY TO JOY

Planning the Session

Session Goals

As a result of conversations and activities connected with this session, group members should begin to

- identify the historical and political setting of the Nativity,
- reflect on the idea of caring for God as a newborn baby,
- understand the role of shepherds in historical and literary context,
- consider the marks of Jesus' Jewish identity, and
- explore the roles of Simeon and Anna in connecting the story of Israel to the story of Jesus.

Scriptural Foundation

In those days Caesar Augustus declared that everyone throughout the empire should be enrolled in the tax lists. This first enrollment occurred when Quirinius governed Syria. Everyone went to their own cities to be enrolled. Since Joseph belonged to David's house and family line, he went

*up from the city of Nazareth in Galilee to David's city, called
Bethlehem, in Judea. He went to be enrolled together with
Mary, who was promised to him in marriage and who was
pregnant. While they were there, the time came for Mary to
have her baby. She gave birth to her firstborn child, a son,
wrapped him snugly, and laid him in a manger, because there
was no place for them in the guestroom.*

*Nearby shepherds were living in the fields, guarding their
sheep at night. The Lord's angel stood before them, the Lord's
glory shone around them, and they were terrified.*

*The angel said, "Don't be afraid! Look! I bring good news to
you—wonderful, joyous news for all people. Your savior is born
today in David's city. He is Christ the Lord. This is a sign for
you: you will find a newborn baby wrapped snugly and lying
in a manger." Suddenly a great assembly of the heavenly forces
was with the angel praising God. They said, "Glory to God in
heaven, and on earth peace among those whom he favors."*

*When the angels returned to heaven, the shepherds said to
each other, "Let's go right now to Bethlehem and see what's
happened. Let's confirm what the Lord has revealed to us."
They went quickly and found Mary and Joseph, and the baby
lying in the manger. When they saw this, they reported what
they had been told about this child. Everyone who heard it
was amazed at what the shepherds told them. Mary committed
these things to memory and considered them carefully. The
shepherds returned home, glorifying and praising God for all
they had heard and seen. Everything happened just as they had
been told.*

*When eight days had passed, Jesus' parents circumcised him
and gave him the name Jesus. This was the name given to him
by the angel before he was conceived. When the time came for
their ritual cleansing, in accordance with the Law from Moses,
they brought Jesus up to Jerusalem to present him to the Lord.*

(It's written in the Law of the Lord, "Every firstborn male will be dedicated to the Lord.") They offered a sacrifice in keeping with what's stated in the Law of the Lord, A pair of turtledoves or two young pigeons.

A man named Simeon was in Jerusalem. He was righteous and devout. He eagerly anticipated the restoration of Israel, and the Holy Spirit rested on him. The Holy Spirit revealed to him that he wouldn't die before he had seen the Lord's Christ. Led by the Spirit, he went into the temple area. Meanwhile, Jesus' parents brought the child to the temple so that they could do what was customary under the Law. Simeon took Jesus in his arms and praised God. He said,

> *"Now, master, let your servant go in peace according to your word,*
> > *because my eyes have seen your salvation.*
> *You prepared this salvation in the presence of all peoples.*
> *It's a light for revelation to the Gentiles and a glory for your people Israel."*

His father and mother were amazed by what was said about him. Simeon blessed them and said to Mary his mother, "This boy is assigned to be the cause of the falling and rising of many in Israel and to be a sign that generates opposition so that the inner thoughts of many will be revealed. And a sword will pierce your innermost being too."

There was also a prophet, Anna the daughter of Phanuel, who belonged to the tribe of Asher. She was very old. After she married, she lived with her husband for seven years. She was now an 84-year-old widow. She never left the temple area but worshipped God with fasting and prayer night and day. She approached at that very moment and began to praise God and to speak about Jesus to everyone who was looking forward to the redemption of Jerusalem.

43

*When Mary and Joseph had completed everything required
by the Law of the Lord, they returned to their hometown,
Nazareth in Galilee. The child grew up and became strong.
He was filled with wisdom, and God's favor was on him.*

Luke 2:1-40

Special Preparation

- Prepare the room with seating arranged in a circle, a semicircle, or at a table so that everyone will be able to see one another.
- Have available paper, pens, pencils, and other drawing materials.
- Have nametags available.
- Also have available large sheets of paper or a whiteboard with markers for writing.
- Provide Bibles for those who may not have brought one.
- Supply a Nativity set with as many pieces as possible.
- On a large piece of paper, create a chart with two columns. Label one column "Matthew" and the other column "Luke." Post the chart in a visible, accessible place in your meeting area.
- On a large piece of paper, write "Shepherds." Post the chart in a visible, accessible place in your meeting area.

Getting Started

Opening Activity

Nativity Scenes

Ask participants to recall how the video sessions so far have included images of a variety of Nativity figurines. Have one or two group members explain the Nativity set.

- What are the essential elements?
- How are they arranged?

- What symbols are included?
- What characters and objects are specific to Luke's story? to Matthew's?

Opening Prayer

Read the following prayer aloud, or use one of your own:

Loving God, God of Joseph and Mary, thank you for choosing to appear to us as a helpless child. Thank you for this time to study with others and learn more about the lives of Mary and Joseph and their journey to Bethlehem. Amen.

Learning Together

Video Study and Discussion

Play the third track on the *Light of the World* DVD: "Session 3: The Journey to Joy" (running time is 9:47 minutes).

After the video session plays, invite discussion and questions from the group. To spark conversation, ask group members to consider this excerpt from the video session and the questions that follow.

> *God wants to be in relationship with us, but relationship has to be a two-way street. Not only does God take care of us, not only does God bring justice and compassion to the world, but we also take care of God, here embodied in this helpless newborn child.*

- Have you ever thought that God wants to be in relationship with you?
- How is the relationship with God a two-way street?
- What other parts of the video stood out to you?
- What did you learn about Luke's Nativity story that you didn't already know?

Book and Bible Study and Discussion

Shepherds

> *Nearby shepherds were living in the fields, guarding their sheep at night. The Lord's angel stood before them, the Lord's glory shone around them, and they were terrified.*
>
> *The angel said, "Don't be afraid! Look! I bring good news to you—wonderful, joyous news for all people. Your savior is born today in David's city. He is Christ the Lord. This is a sign for you: you will find a newborn baby wrapped snugly and lying in a manger." Suddenly a great assembly of the heavenly forces was with the angel praising God. They said, "Glory to God in heaven, and on earth peace among those whom he favors."*
>
> *When the angels returned to heaven, the shepherds said to each other, "Let's go right now to Bethlehem and see what's happened. Let's confirm what the Lord has revealed to us." They went quickly and found Mary and Joseph, and the baby lying in the manger. When they saw this, they reported what they had been told about this child. Everyone who heard it was amazed at what the shepherds told them. Mary committed these things to memory and considered them carefully. The shepherds returned home, glorifying and praising God for all they had heard and seen. Everything happened just as they had been told.*
>
> Luke 2:8-20

Ask the group members to list the characteristics that occur to them when they think of shepherds. Write the responses on the large sheet of paper. Then consider the list together as a group, and compare it to the section on "The Shepherds" in the study book.

- What do the shepherds symbolize in the story of Jesus' birth, and in the larger Christian story?

- How does the angel's appearance to the shepherds compare to the annunciations to Zechariah, Mary, and Joseph?
- Can you recall other shepherds in Scripture (Jacob, Rachel, Moses, David)? What might these connections suggest?
- What does Psalm 23, "The LORD is my shepherd," suggest about the role of shepherds?
- When Jesus refers to himself as the "good shepherd" (John 10:11, 14), what image of Jesus do you have? How is "shepherd" different from "lord" or "father" or "king"?
- The term "pastor" comes from the Latin for "shepherd." (You might make the connection from words like "pastoral" or "pasture.") Do you think of clergy as shepherds? Could anyone take the role of "shepherd"?

Signs

Consider this passage from *Light of the World*. Have a member of the group read it aloud.

> *The sign the shepherds receive is not a supernova or even the angel (which should have been sign enough). It is those bands of cloth, the manger, and the baby. The refusal to offer signs of supernatural status fits within Luke's infancy stories. The sign to Mary was the pregnancy of her cousin Elizabeth. Once we figure out the sign, whether of a pregnant woman, of a mother who has just given birth, of a newborn, even of baby clothes or a stable, our next step is to work out the symbolism, or what that sign "signifies." If we can start to look for the light of the divine in front of our eyes rather than search the stars, we'll be ready when we hear stories of sowers and seeds, vines and fig trees, yeast and fish. Signs are all around us, if we take the time to look.*

- What signs can you identify in the biblical stories you know? Which ones are "supernatural," and which appear in ordinary life?
- AJ writes, "Signs are all around us, if we take the time to look." How does this reflect your own experience?

- Where do we see signs in our ordinary experience? How do we interpret them?
- Describing the shepherds, AJ states, "There is nothing particularly special about what their eyes see; there is everything special about how they interpret what they see." How do the shepherds interpret what they see?
- Why do you think the "sign" is simply a newborn child "wrapped snugly and lying in a manger" (Luke 2:12)?
- How might the shepherds function as a sign to Mary?
- Does having a witness strengthen our own interpretation of what is happening?
- Think of a time when having someone with you helped strengthen your own interpretation of what was happening.

Two Nativities

Talk about the differences in the two Nativity accounts as presented by Matthew and Luke. Ask the group to think about the two stories and list the characteristics of each on the paper divided into two columns labeled "Matthew" and "Luke." Remember the quotation from Session 2's video: "You can have two competing, in fact opposite, views and theologically, you can both be correct."

- How do the differences reflect the authors' different agendas in the Gospels?
- Using only the Nativity stories as a guide, what agenda do you think Luke had in writing? What about Matthew?
- Can you think of how these emphases appear later in each Gospel?

Marking Jewish Identity

When eight days had passed, Jesus' parents circumcised him and gave him the name Jesus. This was the name given to him by the angel before he was conceived. When the time came for their ritual cleansing, in accordance with the Law from Moses, they brought Jesus up to Jerusalem to present him to the Lord.

(It's written in the Law of the Lord, "Every firstborn male will be dedicated to the Lord.") They offered a sacrifice in keeping with what's stated in the Law of the Lord, A pair of turtledoves or two young pigeons.

Luke 2:21-24

Male circumcision is a sign of Jewish identity. Circumcision on the eighth day remains an important ritual in the Jewish tradition. By describing Jesus' circumcision and presentation in the Temple, Luke emphasizes how Mary and Joseph celebrated their membership in the people Israel and celebrated as well that their son continued in the Jewish community.

AJ writes, "Ritual, when performed with full understanding, helps to anchor our identity." Consider the following questions as a group:

- What is the importance of ritual in your life?
- How do the rituals described in Luke 2:21-24 anchor Jesus' Jewish identity?
- How do the infancy stories tell us that human bodies are important and that we should pay attention to them (for example: infertility, the ability to speak, pregnancy, childbirth, circumcision, childcare)?
- How does this concern for bodies show up later in the Gospels (for example: "This is my body," resurrection in the flesh)?
- As Christians, what rituals do we perform to anchor us in our faith? What rituals do we pass along to our children?
- Do we ever take religious ritual for granted, and if so, what might we do to get ourselves back on the right path?

Multiple Perspectives

AJ observes that Luke tells the story of Jesus' conception and birth from Mary's perspective, while Matthew focuses more on Joseph's perspective. Would the story change if we heard it from another character's point of view? Invite participants to choose one of the following characters and briefly jot down a few sentences describing how that character might tell the story.

Shepherds

Angels

Mary

Joseph

The Magi

Herod

Caesar Augustus

Ask the group to respond to the following questions:

- Offer this quotation from AJ's introduction: "We should even celebrate the distinct stories Matthew and Luke offer, since the import of what they recount must be told from multiple perspectives. Something so momentous cannot be contained in a single version." What do you think AJ means by that? What are other examples of important events for which we need multiple versions to understand?
- Do you and members of your family, or friends, have different memories of the same event?
- Can you think of instances where memories differ but the importance of the event remains secure?

Simeon and Anna

Simeon and Anna do not typically take a place in the traditional Nativity account, and yet they play key roles in the celebration of Jesus' birth. AJ writes, "Simeon and Anna, like Zechariah and Elizabeth, represent fidelity to the ancient traditions. We can see them handing on to the next generation, to Mary and Joseph and to the child, the trust that they will guard the stories and practices of the Jewish people."

Invite someone to read Luke 2:25-38 out loud. Then consider the following questions:

- What does Anna do immediately when she sees Jesus? How is this similar to the shepherds' response?
- Why do you think Mary and Joseph were "amazed" by what Simeon was saying?
- Simeon proclaims, "It's a light for revelation to the Gentiles and a glory for your people Israel" (Luke 2:32). What does he mean by this? Can you see places where his proclamation comes true later in the Gospels?
- Simeon further prophesies, "This boy is assigned to be the cause of the falling and rising of many in Israel and to be a sign that generates opposition" (Luke 2:34). What do you think this means? Does it come to pass?
- Finally, Simeon tells Mary, "A sword will pierce your innermost being too" (Luke 2:35). Respond to AJ's reflection on this statement:

The Greek literally says, "A sword will pierce your own soul [psyche]." Jesus is not the only one who will suffer; his mother, letting her son go from her and to his death, will suffer as well. That comment reminds me of John 19:34: "One of the soldiers pierced his side with a spear, and immediately blood and water came out." This description, only in the Gospel of John, hints at Jesus, metaphorically, giving new birth to his followers; it is through the gift of his body that they can be, as he tells Nicodemus, "born anew" or "born from above" (John 3:3, 7 CEB, NRSV). When Jesus dies, John tells us that his mother is at the foot of the cross. And there, she feels the sword and the life draining from her as well.

Wrapping Up

Closing Activity

Jesus' Connection to His People, and God's Fidelity to Israel

Invite the group to consider all the distinctly Jewish aspects of Luke's story of Jesus' birth.

- What are those details?
- How do they connect Jesus to history, to his family, and to his present moment?
- How does knowing about the connection of Jesus' story to the story of ancient Israel, preserved in the Old Testament, help you think about the Old Testament?
- What parts of your own identity—ethnicity, culture, church, and so forth—do you want to pass along to the next generation?

Closing Prayer

Offer the following prayer or one of your own:

Come, Lord Jesus. We give thanks that you came to announce God's good news for the world. Guide us as we seek to encounter you in Scripture and in our interactions with one another. Grant us the courage to say yes to the difficult challenges we face in our own lives, now and forever. Amen.

Session 4

THE GIFTS OF THE GENTILES

Planning the Session

Session Goals

As a result of conversations and activities connected with this session, group members should begin to

- understand the different emphases in Luke's and Matthew's stories of Jesus' birth,
- appreciate Matthew's genealogy as a theological meditation and not just a list of names,
- reflect on the role of prophecy and the connection of the two Testaments,
- understand the place of the Magi in historical and literary context, and
- see how for Luke and Matthew, knowing the political contexts adds richness to their Gospels.

Scriptural Foundation

This is how the birth of Jesus Christ took place. When Mary his mother was engaged to Joseph, before they were married, she became pregnant by the Holy Spirit. Joseph her husband was a righteous man. Because he didn't want to humiliate her, he decided to call off their engagement quietly. As he was thinking about this, an angel from the Lord appeared to him in a dream and said, "Joseph son of David, don't be afraid to take Mary as your wife, because the child she carries was conceived by the Holy Spirit. She will give birth to a son, and you will call him Jesus, because he will save his people from their sins." Now all of this took place so that what the Lord had spoken through the prophet would be fulfilled:

> *Look! A virgin will become pregnant and give birth to a son,*
> > *And they will call him, Emmanuel.*

(Emmanuel means "God with us.")

When Joseph woke up, he did just as an angel from God commanded and took Mary as his wife. But he didn't have sexual relations with her until she gave birth to a son. Joseph called him Jesus.

After Jesus was born in Bethlehem in the territory of Judea during the rule of King Herod, magi came from the east to Jerusalem. They asked, "Where is the newborn king of the Jews? We've seen his star in the east, and we've come to honor him."

When King Herod heard this, he was troubled, and everyone in Jerusalem was troubled with him. He gathered all the chief priests and the legal experts and asked them where the Christ was to be born. They said, "In Bethlehem of Judea, for this is what the prophet wrote:

> *You, Bethlehem, land of Judah,*
> > *by no means are you least among the rulers of Judah,*
> > > *because from you will come one who governs,*
> > > *who will shepherd my people Israel."*

Then Herod secretly called for the magi and found out from them the time when the star had first appeared. He sent them to Bethlehem, saying, "Go and search carefully for the child. When you've found him, report to me so that I too may go and honor him." When they heard the king, they went; and look, the star they had seen in the east went ahead of them until it stood over the place where the child was. When they saw the star, they were filled with joy. They entered the house and saw the child with Mary his mother. Falling to their knees, they honored him. Then they opened their treasure chests and presented him with gifts of gold, frankincense, and myrrh. Because they were warned in a dream not to return to Herod, they went back to their own country by another route.

When the magi had departed, an angel from the Lord appeared to Joseph in a dream and said, "Get up. Take the child and his mother and escape to Egypt. Stay there until I tell you, for Herod will soon search for the child in order to kill him." Joseph got up and, during the night, took the child and his mother to Egypt. He stayed there until Herod died. This fulfilled what the Lord had spoken through the prophet: I have called my son out of Egypt.

Matthew 1:18–2:15

Special Preparation

- Prepare the room with seating arranged in a circle, a semicircle, or at a table so that everyone will be able to see one another.
- Have available paper, pens, pencils, and other drawing materials.
- Have nametags available.
- Also have available large sheets of paper or a whiteboard with markers for writing.
- Provide Bibles for those who may not have brought one.

Getting Started

Opening Activity

Family Trees

Both Matthew and Luke include genealogies for Jesus (Matthew 1:1-16 and Luke 3:23-38). Matthew traces Jesus' origins beginning with Abraham and concluding with, "Jacob was the father of Joseph, the husband of Mary—of whom Jesus was born, who is called the Christ" (1:16). We'll hear more on the particularities of Matthew's genealogy in this session. Luke begins with "son of Joseph" (3:23) and works backward, arriving at "son of Adam son of God" (3:38).

- With the advent of new technology such as Ancestry.com and 23andme, how and why are we interested in tracing our own genealogies?
- Why do Matthew and Luke think it is important to present lists of Jesus' ancestors?
- Have you ever made your own family tree? What did you learn about yourself? What purpose did it serve?
- Where else in the Bible do we see genealogies? (See, for example: Genesis 5:1-32, Genesis 10, Ruth 4:18-22, 1 Chronicles 1–10, Judith 8:1.) Do we tend to overlook them? What do we lose if we ignore them?

Opening Prayer

Read the following prayer aloud, or use one of your own:

Eternal God of love, as we enter these final days of Advent, gather us together into a place of quiet rest. Here in this place, prepare for us a space in which we can contemplate the gifts of the Advent season. Guide us as we seek to find ways to give you thanks for your love, and help us discern how best to respond. Amen.

Learning Together

Video Study and Discussion

Play the fourth track on the *Light of the World* DVD: "Session 4: The Gifts of the Gentiles" (running time is 13:04 minutes).

After the video session plays, invite discussion and questions from the group. To spark conversation, ask group members to consider this excerpt from the video session and the questions that follow.

> *Joseph had been warned in a dream to take the baby and flee to Egypt. Jesus survives when children around him are slaughtered. What would that have meant to him, personally, knowing that other people died, and he lived? What responsibility does he have? And then, what responsibility do we who tell the story have?*

- How would you answer these questions for Jesus? for yourself?
- Do we have responsibility to respond to events in our own history?
- What other parts of the video stood out to you?
- What did you learn about the Magi that you didn't already know?

Bible Study and Discussion

Women in Matthew's Genealogy

Read together as a group or have several people read out loud Matthew 1:1-17. Enjoy the experience of trying to pronounce all the names!

As you read, stop every time a woman's name is mentioned. Notice how she is identified and how this identification breaks the rhythm of the genealogical list. Name the women: Tamar, Rahab, Ruth, wife of Uriah, and Mary. For each woman mentioned, call for the class to say who she is, what she did, and why she might be on the list.

- The women are not the matriarchs you might expect to find in a genealogy: Sarah, Rebecca, Leah, and Rachel. Why do you think Matthew mentions this particular group of women?
- How do they reflect that the good news is also going to gentiles?
- In what ways do these women anticipate Mary and her situation?

Caught in Adultery?

Have a member of the group read Matthew 1:18-25 aloud, and consider the questions that follow. Then do the same with the next passage, John 8:1-11.

> *This is how the birth of Jesus Christ took place. When Mary his mother was engaged to Joseph, before they were married, she became pregnant by the Holy Spirit. Joseph her husband was a righteous man. Because he didn't want to humiliate her, he decided to call off their engagement quietly. As he was thinking about this, an angel from the Lord appeared to him in a dream and said, "Joseph son of David, don't be afraid to take Mary as your wife, because the child she carries was conceived by the Holy Spirit. She will give birth to a son, and you will call him Jesus, because he will save his people from their sins." Now all of this took place so that what the Lord had spoken through the prophet would be fulfilled:*
>
> > Look! A virgin will become pregnant and give birth to a son,
> > And they will call him, *Emmanuel.*
>
> (Emmanuel *means "God with us."*)
>
> *When Joseph woke up, he did just as an angel from God commanded and took Mary as his wife. But he didn't have sexual relations with her until she gave birth to a son. Joseph called him Jesus.*
>
> *Matthew 1:18-25*

- When you first heard this story growing up, how many of you perceived that Mary's life was in danger because of this situation or that Joseph saved her from being stoned? Did it surprise you to learn that this was not the case?
- What happens when personal concerns become public?
- Do you think that women and men are held to double standards in matters of personal behavior?

Now read:

And Jesus went to the Mount of Olives. Early in the morning he returned to the temple. All the people gathered around him, and he sat down and taught them. The legal experts and Pharisees brought a woman caught in adultery. Placing her in the center of the group, they said to Jesus, "Teacher, this woman was caught in the act of committing adultery. In the Law, Moses commanded us to stone women like this. What do you say?" They said this to test him, because they wanted a reason to bring an accusation against him. Jesus bent down and wrote on the ground with his finger.

They continued to question him, so he stood up and replied, "Whoever hasn't sinned should throw the first stone." Bending down again, he wrote on the ground. Those who heard him went away, one by one, beginning with the elders. Finally, only Jesus and the woman were left in the middle of the crowd.

Jesus stood up and said to her, "Woman, where are they? Is there no one to condemn you?"

She said, "No one, sir."

Jesus said, "Neither do I condemn you. Go, and from now on, don't sin anymore."

John 8:1-11

- What light does the story in John 8 shed on Mary's situation? What questions does it raise?

- How does knowing that stoning was not, as far as we can tell, being practiced at the time as a response to adultery or infidelity change your understanding of Joseph's actions?
- AJ writes, "One does not need to invent a negative image of Judaism in order to see the grace of the Christmas story." What does she mean?

Isaiah's Prophecy

Have someone read each of the following two passages out loud:

"Therefore, the Lord will give you a sign. The young woman is pregnant and is about to give birth to a son, and she will name him Immanuel."

Isaiah 7:14

Now all of this took place so that what the Lord had spoken through the prophet would be fulfilled:

Look! A virgin will become pregnant and give birth to a son,
   And they will call him, *Emmanuel.*

(Emmanuel *means "God with us."*)

When Joseph woke up, he did just as an angel from God commanded and took Mary as his wife. But he didn't have sexual relations with her until she gave birth to a son. Joseph called him Jesus.

Matthew 1:22-23

- What are the differences between the two verses? Note words and verb tense, among other details. How does the study book explain these differences?
- Does it change your perception of the Christmas story knowing that the original Hebrew prophecy uses the term "young woman" and not "virgin"?

- AJ writes, "There is little reason to argue over who has the correct reading here. Isaiah's words will mean, and should mean, different things to different people over time." Do you agree or disagree with her?
- If we see Jesus to have fulfilled a prophecy, does that mean that the prophecy no longer has anything to say?
- What does "God with us" suggest to you? Do you read the story differently knowing that the last line of Matthew's Gospel is, "Look, I myself will be with you every day until the end of this present age"?

Who Are the Magi?

Have someone read out loud the story of the Magi in Matthew 2.

After Jesus was born in Bethlehem in the territory of Judea during the rule of King Herod, magi came from the east to Jerusalem. They asked, "Where is the newborn king of the Jews? We've seen his star in the east, and we've come to honor him."

When King Herod heard this, he was troubled, and everyone in Jerusalem was troubled with him. He gathered all the chief priests and the legal experts and asked them where the Christ was to be born. They said, "In Bethlehem of Judea, for this is what the prophet wrote:

> *You, Bethlehem, land of Judah,*
> > *by no means are you least among the rulers of Judah,*
> > *because from you will come one who governs,*
> > *who will shepherd my people Israel."*

Then Herod secretly called for the magi and found out from them the time when the star had first appeared. He sent them to Bethlehem, saying, "Go and search carefully for the child. When you've found him, report to me so that I too may go and

honor him." *When they heard the king, they went; and look,
the star they had seen in the east went ahead of them until
it stood over the place where the child was. When they saw
the star, they were filled with joy. They entered the house and
saw the child with Mary his mother. Falling to their knees,
they honored him. Then they opened their treasure chests and
presented him with gifts of gold, frankincense, and myrrh.
Because they were warned in a dream not to return to Herod,
they went back to their own country by another route.*

Matthew 2:1-12

- Who are the Magi? What are they coming to Bethlehem
  to do? Why?
- Do we imagine them at the stable? Or at Joseph and Mary's
  home in Bethlehem, where Mary was perhaps nursing Jesus or
  changing his diaper, as AJ imagines in the video session?
- What does Herod tell the Magi to do? Why don't they do it?
- AJ writes, "Matthew presents the Magi, who, despite 'we three
  kings of Orient are,' are not necessarily three, not necessarily
  all men, certainly not kings, and most certainly not wise." How
  does her description of the Magi (filled out in more detail in the
  study book) change your perception of them?

Thinking Ahead

Throughout *Light of the World*, AJ emphasizes the importance
of considering the Nativity stories in their larger contexts: that of the
Gospels, the Old Testament, the historical setting, the entirety of both
testaments, and subsequent interpretation. The Nativity stories contain
not only details about the birth of Jesus but also symbols and references
that point us to his life and ministry.

Have a member of the group read the following passage out loud:

*We can, and should, savor each event individually, but we
should also appreciate them as connected into a larger whole. We
cannot fully understand the Annunciation until we have witnessed*

the birth; we cannot fully understand the birth until we have walked with Jesus from Galilee to Jerusalem, and we cannot fully understand this journey until we have gone to the cross, the tomb, Emmaus, and back to Jerusalem.

- How do the Nativity stories function in the larger story of the Gospels?
- What aspects of Luke and Matthew's Nativity stories prepare us for Jesus' future?

Readers and Historians

Upon learning about the details of the Nativity accounts, some people want to point out the discrepancies in order to discredit the entire tradition. AJ finds this move to be inappropriate. She writes, "Our role as historians is to ask, 'What would these stories have conveyed to the people who first heard them?' Our role as readers is also to ask, 'What do these stories mean to me, and what have they meant to my community and to my tradition over time and across the globe?'"

Divide the class into two groups. With regard to the Nativity stories in Matthew and Luke, ask the "historians" to consider the first question, and the "readers" to think about the second. Have each group write responses on a large sheet of paper. Bring the groups back together and display their lists side by side. Where is there overlap? For responses that don't overlap, talk about how those are particular and complementary.

Wrapping Up

Closing Activity

Reconsidering the Events of the Nativity Stories

As in the first session, ask the group members to share, without looking in the study book or a Bible, the events around Jesus' birth as they can remember them. Write their responses on a large piece of paper posted where everyone can see. After a few minutes, post the similar list from the first session and examine the differences. Ask the group:

- What differences do you see between the two lists?
- What do you make of these differences?
- How does knowing more about the events around Jesus' birth enhance your faith?
- What new details in this study challenged or enriched your understanding of these events?
- What did you learn in this study that meant the most to you?
- What else now do you want to know?
- Finally, ask the group: If you could ask AJ three questions, what would you ask her?

Closing Prayer

If the group is using a common biblical translation, invite them to read aloud Isaiah 40:31. Alternatively, ask a member of the group to read it aloud.

> *Those who hope in the LORD*
> *will renew their strength;*
> *they will fly up on wings like eagles;*
> *they will run and not be tired;*
> *they will walk and not be weary.*
> Isaiah 40:31

God, our Lord. As the light of Christmas dawns and begins to shine fully, we give thanks for the gift and hope of Jesus Christ. Let us remember the Nativity in all its rich detail and appreciate the fullness of the story of Christ's birth seen from every perspective. Guide us as we move through the Christmas season, and into the world with the Advent gifts of hope, love, joy, and peace. Amen.

CPSIA information can be obtained
at www.ICGtesting.com
Printed in the USA
LVHW082123311019
636001LV00004B/4/P